$1 — 10/23

D0810597

hex
appeal

hex
appeal

Seductive spells for the sassy sorceress

Lucy Summers

Illustrations by Lucy Truman

A QUARTO BOOK

First edition for North America published in 2004
by Barron's Educational Series, Inc.

Copyright © 2004 by Quarto Inc.

All inquiries should be addressed to:
Barron's Educational Series, Inc.
250 Wireless Boulevard
Hauppauge, NY 11788
http://www.barronseduc.com
International Standard Book Number
0-7641-5786-8
Library of Congress Catalog Card Number
2004103637

QUAR.HAP

Conceived, designed, and produced by
Quarto Publishing plc
The Old Brewery
6 Blundell Street
London N7 9BH

Project Editor Jo Fisher
Art Editor and Designer Katie Eke
Designer Louise Clements
Assistant Art Director Penny Cobb
Copy Editor Claire Waite Brown
Photographer Colin Bowling
Illustrators Lucy Truman
Proof reader Sally Maceachern
Indexer Pamela Ellis

Art Director Moira Clinch
Publisher Piers Spence

Manufactured by Universal Graphics, Singapore
Printed by Midas Printing International Ltd, China

Contents

Loving & hexing
in the 21st Century

Magic is the mysterious, invisible, and powerful energy that connects us to every other being and thing on the planet, and as such is a useful ally in affairs of the heart. Love, and the need to share our life with someone special, is a strong human drive. Most of us can survive happily alone, if that is what we choose at the time. However, you only have to look at the number of personal contact ads and dating agencies out there, and consider the sudden growth in Internet chat rooms and the speed-dating phenomenon to realize that a great many people also fear loneliness. The truth of the matter is that we all want someone else—someone special—who we can love and cherish, and who will love and cherish us back. This is probably why, of all the things magic can be used for, love magic captures the popular imagination the most.

What is magic?

Magic is beyond description—and probably beyond all current forms of scientific investigation. Like most kinds of energy, magic has its own rules and ways of being manipulated, and those using spellcraft learn how to use this energy, how to increase its natural power, and how other factors may disrupt it. Learning to manipulate magical energy in this way is not difficult, it simply takes a little practice, imagination, and patience. In fact, most people use simple magic every day, whether by wishing, saying prayers, or even sending someone a "get well" card. These are all examples of one basic principle of magic, the desire to alter current circumstances.

Why should I try love magic?

Using magic to bring love into your life or to solve relationship problems can be very effective. This is because our emotions are involved, serving to strengthen our desires and our will to succeed—vital to the working of spells. When you understand that magic is within you, and you learn to believe in its power, you can make all manner of positive changes to your own life and emotions, and those of the most important people in your life.

How do spells work?

Magic is an invisible force that connects and permeates everything. Every thought and action you have will affect this force, like a ripple on a pond. This means that magical energy can be influenced and directed toward a designated purpose by using certain means. The most important of these "means" is your will. The more you want something to happen and the more clearly you can visualize the outcome, the stronger the spell will be. Like any craft, this takes practice. But eventually you will actually "feel" the energies as they flow around you, and be able to work with them instinctively.

However, not all spells will work. Magical energy can be influenced by outside forces, things other than your will. For example, the will of the person your spell is directed at may be stronger than your desire to succeed. Destiny can also help or hinder your magic. So, if your spell doesn't seem to work, don't immediately blame your lack of prowess, you may simply be using the wrong magic at the wrong time.

What else do I need to cast spells?

To help your spells succeed, you can employ helpers to act as "boosters" to the magical purpose of the spell. These "ingredients" are chosen to be in sympathy with the purpose of the particular spell and contain energies of their own that enhance the power of the magic. For example, specific magical energies can be evoked by carrying out a spell on a particular day of the week, or by using a certain herb (see pages 120-123). The spells in this book use a variety of helpers:

An altar

A small altar is used in many of the spells in this book. It serves as a focal point for your magical workings as well as a handy place to put lit candles, incense, and other ingredients. You could try using a coffee table, a wooden packing crate, or even an old cardboard box (though make sure it's stable!).

Candles

Fire energy increases the power of any spell and candle flames are also a great aid to focusing on what you want. Colored candles help to focus the energy for whatever purpose the color is in sympathy with. It is always useful to have a good supply of various candles. Even if you don't use them for magic, they are a must for creating romantic atmospheres.

Chants

Chants help to focus the mind on your purpose. The words of the chants in this book do not contain any power in their own right, but they do help to increase your own power by suggestion.

Colors, days of the week, directions, and elements

All of these relate to different energies that are useful for various types of spells.

Crystals and stones

Crystals can act like "transmitters" and "amplifiers" of your will—as long as it is in sympathy with the crystal's energy. Some stones and certain crystals also have receptive powers, which means they can absorb energy and hold it in until cleansed, which is very useful in protective magic.

Essential oils

Essential oils are oils distilled from plants, flowers, barks, and resins. They contain the plant's subtle energies in much the same way as fresh or dried plant material. However, as the oils are concentrated, you need to use less than plant material in other forms. Oils are useful for anointing candles and other objects, as well as adding to spell mixtures.

Gods and goddesses

Although some of the spells use the names of gods or goddesses associated with love, they have purposely been avoided where possible. This is because not all spellcasters follow Wicca or any other pagan path. However, if you wish to insert the name of a god or goddess in the spells because you feel it is right for you, go ahead.

Incense

Different scents have their own specific vibrations. Lifted up on incense smoke, your spell is carried out into the wider universe.

Herbs and flowers

Many herbs, flowers, and trees contain gentle yet effective energies and they are usually simple to obtain.

Pouches

Many spells use pouches of certain colors and materials to "contain" the magic. You could make up some of these beforehand, or at least collect fabric swatches to make them from. It is always preferable to use material that hasn't been used or worn before, but if that isn't possible, don't worry too much.

Symbols

Symbols have been used in magic for thousands of years. As such they contain the accumulated energies not only of their own forms, but also of continued magical use. Therefore, although they appear as flat, two-dimensional objects, their application can add power to a spell.

How do I find the ingredients?

All the ingredients used in the spells in this book are available from grocery stores, pharmacies, health food suppliers, by mail order, or on the Internet. Searching for the rarer ingredients will lend an extra focus to the intention of the spell.

If you collect any materials from the wild, please have respect for the environment and any local conservation laws. When taking wild plants, do not take them all from one spot; ask permission from the plant spirits, and leave something behind as a token of thanks—even simply a hair from your head.

If, despite your best efforts, you are unable to obtain an ingredient, it is fine to substitute it with something else, just as long as it contains the same energy vibration (see pages 120-123). In extreme cases you could always leave it out, but of course this will decrease the overall power of the spell.

What are the ethics of spellcasting?

Magical energy, in itself, is neutral, it is the purpose to which it is put that makes it either good or bad magic. All good spellcasters and witches steer well clear of the latter, and believe that what they give out will return to them three times over. However, there is much magic that occupies the middle ground between out-and-out good magic and magic for selfish or harmful intentions. Love magic often falls into this middle ground, because it involves another person. It is recommended, before casting a spell, that you consider the situation with a truthful—and not just a wishful—eye, and weigh whether you are willing to take any bad karma that may result.

It should be remembered that love not freely given, is not really love at all, but an illusion that will, in the long run, not last. It is far better to perform a spell that deepens a friendship first. Who knows what may happen then? But we are only human and love is a powerful force. Therefore, spells have been included that may speed things up a bit while lessening any possible fallout. Finally, destiny also plays a large part in love: what will be, will be. If you are truly not meant to be together in this lifetime, then all the magic spells in the world will be powerless in the face of such a strong universal force.

Are there any precautions I should take?

✳ None of the spells in this book could summon harmful forces. Nevertheless, it is recommended that anyone with mental illness should not practice magic without experienced guidance.

✳ Pregnant women should not handle the herbs or essential oils mentioned in this book without first seeking medical advice.

✳ Always make sure that candles and incense sticks are placed away from flammable materials and that items are burned in a safe place.

✳ Never leave a lit candle unattended.

✳ Apart from these few precautions, the spells are both safe and simple to use, not to mention effective!

Sexy
seductress
makeovers

Do you need to do a little work on yourself before working magic on others? Well, never fear. From head to toe, prepare yourself to be the most fabulous female around with these magical potions and lotions. And if that isn't enough, give yourself some glamor, slap on some self-confidence, and learn to dance like a diva. When you've put yourself through these marvelous magical makeovers, you can be sure that you'll be the most enchanting temptress around!

?Q: What can I do to boost my self-confidence?

A: **Few people are confident all the time,** and some are so lacking in self-esteem that it becomes crippling, affecting every social engagement they attend. Catty comments from others can worsen the situation. If this is you, you need to boost your self-image and rise above the negativity of others by constantly reinforcing your mind with positive images. This mind magic will help you become the dynamic person you know you were always meant to be.

Make up a necklace of seven crystal beads using jewelry thread and clasps. Make sure all the knots are secure. Take a sheet of parchment paper and, taking great care with your handwriting and making no mistakes, **write the following positive affirmations:**

I am a beautiful person, both inside and out
I am a pleasure to be with
I am a strong and confident woman
I am full of intelligent conversation
I am not afraid to be myself
I am happy and fulfilled
I am blessed by the universe

If you wish, you can add extra designs to the parchment, in various colors, to make it more special. At bedtime, take the parchment and the necklace to a place where you can sit quietly and undisturbed in front of a mirror.

Facing yourself in the mirror, hold the necklace and rub a different bead while repeating each of the affirmations on the parchment. Say each one with determination and meaning and visualize yourself becoming the person you've always wanted to be. When you have finished, roll up the parchment and wrap the necklace around it. Store the charm in a safe and

easy-to-reach place. Repeat this recitation with the beads and mirror every night for at least a month and you'll experience a vast increase in your self-confidence. Use them again in the same way whenever you need a boost. You could also wear the necklace whenever you go out to remind yourself of your magic.

CHECKLIST

Best to use: At the time of the waxing moon, but can be used anytime you have a confidence crisis.

How often: Whenever you need a boost to your self-esteem. With this magic, it won't be too often!

You will need:
7 crystal beads, preferably tiger's eye
Jewelry thread and clasps
A sheet of parchment paper
A pen
A mirror

Q: Is there any way I can give myself a radiant glow?

A: **When you see someone whose skin** seems to glow with an inner light, you just know she's going to attract the best men. So why not equal the odds with this special potion that captures the qualities of sunlight and love magic? You will need to test the potion on a very small patch of skin before splashing it all over, to make sure you are not allergic to any of the ingredients.

Place the flowers and herbs in a bowl and cover them with boiling water. Leave to cool, then strain the herbs from the water, which has now been infused with their essence. Add 13 drops of dew and a citrine crystal to the infusion and store the potion in a refrigerator. Leave for 12 hours to allow the citrine crystal to lend its sunny power to the blend.

Remove the crystal and apply a little of the potion to a small area of skin. Leave for 12 hours to ensure you do not react to any of the ingredients.

To use the potion all over, wash your face and body as always, then splash the mixture over your skin, leaving it to dry naturally.

CHECKLIST
Best to use: First thing in the morning.
How often: You can use this as often as you like, as long as you remember to make a fresh mixture every few days.

You will need:
- A handful of calendula petals
- A handful of rose petals
- A handful of chamomile flowers
- A handful of rosemary
- Morning dew, gathered with a heavy cloth left out overnight, then wrung into a container
- A citrine crystal

Repeat the process over the next few days and your skin should take on the sunshine qualities of the ingredients, and will radiate that beautiful fresh glow you've always wanted.

Store the potion, without the crystal, in the fridge. Bear in mind though that this mixture does not have a long shelf life and will need to be replaced with a fresh batch every four to five days. Before it can be used again, the citrine crystal needs to be washed then recharged by placing it in sunlight for one day.

?Q: How can I make sure I'm dressed to thrill?

A: **So, the party's approaching fast** and you still don't know what to wear. All you are certain about is that you want to be an instant hit and make a lasting impression, especially on all the available men you know are going to be there. Don't panic—simply use this spell to guide your feet to the best little sexy party number in town.

To make the seeking oil, combine a teaspoon of almond oil and two drops of vanilla oil with one drop each of cypress and sandalwood essential oils in a dark glass bottle. Put the top on the bottle and shake it well to mix the oils thoroughly. Do a patch test on a very small area of skin and leave it on for 12 hours, to make sure you are not allergic to any of the ingredients.

Just before you are about to go shopping, light a green candle and sit in front of it, making sure you will not be disturbed. Allow your mind to drift and think about all the outfits you've looked hot in in the past. Then think about the sort of impression you'd like to make at the party. Imagine the style that suits you and your preferred color. When you have a clear picture in your mind of your ideal outfit, take the oil and rub it onto the soles of your bare feet while **saying the following charm:**

*I shall seek and I shall find
With magic's aid, all shall be clear
    This charm shall all wishes bind
    And bring my outfit ever near*

*I shall seek and not be tired
    I will have the best of times
And soon the clothes I desire
    Shall be mine, shall be mine.*

*I shall seek and find my way
Through every shop on every street
    Until I find the clothes I want
Guided by my magic feet*

With magical "wings" on your feet you can now "fly" to the boutiques, confident that the right clothes are just waiting for you to come and claim them!

CHECKLIST

Best to use: Just before your shopping trip and preferably on a Thursday during the waxing moon.

How often: No more than once a month.

You will need:

- Almond oil
- Vanilla oil
- Cypress essential oil
- Sandalwood essential oil
- A dark glass bottle with a top
- A green candle

?Q: How can I make my hair more beautiful?

A: **Men love beautiful hair** so it makes sense to do everything you can to enhance this asset. Diet and environment play a major role in the way hair looks, so make sure you eat plenty of fruit and vegetables, drink lots of water, and stay out of the sun. But apart from that, there are other things you can do to add luster to your locks. You could certainly do worse than try this hair rinse made from fruit. I call it Aphrodite's Amazing Hair Enhancer.

Peel an apple, an orange, and a slice of watermelon but don't throw away the peel. Put 2 pints (1.2 l) of spring water into a saucepan and add the fruit and the peel, as well as three sprigs of rosemary.

Bring to the boil. Once the water is boiling, cover the saucepan and leave to simmer for about ten minutes before turning off the heat. Leave the mixture to stand for three hours before straining and discarding the fruit. Add 2 pints (1.2 l) of cider vinegar to the resulting infusion and pour into a bottle. You will need to let the ingredients settle for a couple of days before use.

To make your hair shiny and scented with fruit, add ½ pint (300 ml) to the final rinse water after washing your hair with your usual shampoo.

CHECKLIST

Best to use: When you want your hair to look amazing.

How often: As often as you wash your hair.

You will need:

An apple
An orange
Spring water
A small slice of
  watermelon
Fresh rosemary
Cider vinegar
A saucepan with a cover
A bottle with a top

$_?$Q: How can I make myself irresistible to anyone?

A: **Using an age-old magical technique** of creating an aura of glamor around yourself, you can and will be attractive to everyone. In its original old Scottish context, the word "glamor" means a magic spell or charm, so when you perform this act of magic, you will be carrying on an ancient tradition.

This spell is best performed at midnight, just before the full moon. Set up an altar with a small weaving loom standing propped up in the center, surrounded by three incense sticks. Position two purple candles and a goddess figurine at the back. After bathing and putting on clean clothing, light the candles and incense sticks and kneel before the altar. **Say:**

> *Beloved goddess who rules the heart*
> *Aid me in this magic art*
> *When blessed smoke this room shall wreathe*
> *From its patterns I shall weave*
> *A cloak o'enchantment, fit for a queen*
> *A cloak so fine, that it can't be seen*
> *A cloak of power, a cloak of glamor,*
> *A cloak of love, that shall enamor*
> *When this cloak I shall wear*
> *Everyone shall find me fair.*

Pass your hands through the incense smoke and over the loom and visualize yourself weaving this wondrous cloak. In your mind's eye, see the magical warp and weft forming a sparkling, semitransparent fabric that glitters with the light of a thousand dreams. Now carefully take your magical cloak of glamor and place it around your shoulders. Immediately feel the difference as you take on the irresistible power of magical attraction. Imagine that each time you wear the cloak everyone is pulled toward you in love and admiration. When you take the cloak off, place it carefully in a box and keep it in a special place so that you know where it is whenever you need it. Be careful though about the company in which you choose to don it, otherwise you may attract every love rat in town!

CHECKLIST

Best to use: Whenever you are going out and want to attract a mate.

How often: Whenever necessary but don't abuse its power.

You will need:
- A child's weaving loom, set up
- A sandalwood, a patchouli, and a rose incense stick and 3 incense stick holders
- 2 purple candles
- A goddess figurine
- A cloak-sized box

?Q: Can I learn to dance more sexily?

A: **Sexy dancing has been used** throughout history to captivate and enchant potential mates. Even if you don't think you could ever be a Beyoncé or a Kylie, you can still learn to move in a way guaranteed to make any red-blooded male hot under the collar. Do not expect a quick fix, though. To be able to move well, you must first learn to be comfortable in your own body and this takes a bit of practice—so dust off that leotard and those leggings!

To begin with, seek out a local class that encourages you to move your body. This could be anything from salsa to yoga, but the ones I recommend are belly dancing and Argentinian tango. Don't expect too much of yourself at first, and don't allow yourself to be embarrassed by your mistakes—everyone will be making them, even if you aren't aware of it.

Second, practice movement in the privacy of your own home. For this you will need a full-length mirror, to help you see which moves work best. Make your practice a sacred ritual—after all, dance has long been used in spiritual ceremonies. Light a candle and some incense, and wear the clothes that make you feel the most sexy. Have the music ready, something you enjoy and that you think you will move well to. Begin by sitting quietly in front of the candle and uttering a prayer to the tantric deities Shakti and Shiva. Both are associated with dance and love.

CHECKLIST

Best to use: On the night of a full moon, and if it's a Friday, all the better!

How often: You can practice the dancing anytime but use this ritual only once a month—if necessary.

You will need:
A full-length mirror
A candle
Incense sticks
Music

Now begin moving slowly to the music. Practice letting go of your inhibitions—don't forget, no one else can see you! Watch the way you move in the mirror. To finish, blow out the candle and thank Shakti and Shiva. Keep up the practice and you'll be the sexiest mover on the floor!

Shakti, lend me your dancing feet
That I might touch the ecstasy of spirit.
Shiva, lord of the dance,
Show me how to move my body.
Teach me release
Teach me expression
Teach me the passion
That I should learn to be whole.

Getting
your guy

Whether you have already seen the man of your dreams or are still searching for your soul mate, it's time to wave that magic wand of attraction and lure him into your arms. Whatever type of man lights your fire, you are only a spell away from made-to-order paradise. And if you're not sure that he's the right one for you, find out using a spot of divination. Then, when you've hooked him, make sure that your first date is one to remember by creating the most enchanting first impression!

Q: How can I attract a soul mate?

A: **Soul mates are those with whom** we feel a deep connection that cannot easily be explained. Many psychics and mediums see soul mates as people with whom we have shared many lifetimes, in various types of relationships. Needless to say, then, we can have more than one soul mate alive on earth at any one time, and not all soul mates bring good energies with them. However, most of us feel the need to find a person we regard as "the one," a person who will love us as deeply as we love them. This spell is designed to bring that person into your life.

Perform this spell a few days before the full moon, on either a Wednesday or a Friday. Set up a small altar and place everything you need for the spell on it. Light the two candles and incense. Sit still for a few minutes and calm your mind. Sense a loving presence out there in the darkness, a presence you know, waiting to be called in. When the feeling is strong, place a lock of your hair, a photograph of yourself, a gold ring, and a vanilla pod into a deep pink velvet or silk pouch and **say:**

As moth to night-scented bloom　　*That guides you here*
As bee to flower　　*It is the time and I am calling*
As night follows day　　*It is the time and I am calling*
As sun chases moon　　*I draw you in*
As minutes fill hour　　*I draw you in*
Hear my call　　*I draw you in*
O love of my heart　　*I bring you home.*
Follow the light

Wind the tie of the pouch around the neck of the pouch to close it. Then tie seven knots, **saying as you do so:**

One to call that he may hear
Two to bring his footsteps near
Three to meet
And four to greet

Five for love's sweet seeds to grow
Six, a lifetime of bliss to know
And the seventh shall seal it
It is so.

Hang the pouch above your bed and wherever your soul mate is, he shall soon be drawn to you.

CHECKLIST

Best to use: As close to the full moon as possible and either on a Wednesday or a Friday.

How often: Once only—and have patience.

You will need:
2 deep pink candles
A patchouli incense stick and an incense stick holder
A lock of your hair
A small photograph of yourself
A gold ring
A vanilla pod
A deep pink velvet or silk pouch with a tie

Q: There is someone I particularly want. How can I make him notice me?

A: **So you've seen this really cute guy** and you would like to get to know him better. The problem is, he doesn't seem to know you exist. Well, you can either dance on the table in front of him as he's sipping his cappuccino, or you could try this attraction spell. As with most love spells, you cannot compel someone to come to you if they really don't want to, but the spell will open up the right energies between you, creating the necessary atmosphere for love. A little homework is required as you need to have something that has been in contact with him. Of course, the ideal item would be some of his hair, or a piece of clothing. But if these seem impossible, collect some dust or soil from ground that he has walked on.

Place something from the man you have your eye on into a bowl of spring water and leave it in sunlight for seven days, so that the water can absorb his energy, or essence. At the end of the seven days, decant the water into a small bottle with a top and place it in your purse.

When you see him again, put a little of the water on your finger and surreptitiously dab it onto your heart and third eye chakras. Imagine a pink light stretching from your heart chakra to his and under your breath repeat the following **chant:**

Heart to heart and eye to eye
You and I should play "I-spy."
Eye to eye and heart to heart
Let this thing between us start.

It won't hurt to let him notice you looking at him, but don't stare too obviously or for too long; he'll just think you're crazy. On the other hand, a shy, flirtatious glance before looking away will intrigue him, and, pulled by the power of the spell, will make him want to get to know you better.

CHECKLIST

Best to use: As close to the new moon as possible and choose a week when there will be sunny days.

How often: Use this spell just the once for any one man.

You will need:

Something from the man in question

Spring water

A bottle with a top, small enough to fit in your purse

Q: How can I make guys swarm around me like bees to honey?

A. To attract a bevy of beautiful young men, forget about bees and honey and instead become a spider, entrapping them, like flies, in your cunningly woven web of seduction. Then, of course, you'll have the pick of a number of eligible prospects.

Measure out a 9 foot (2.7 m) length of red cotton thread. Cut this and lay it to one side with some beads. Light two red candles and place them in front of you. Kneel in front of the candles and hold up your hands in front of you, palms facing forward in prayer. **Say:**

> *Great goddesses of love and seduction—Venus, Hathor, Aphrodite, Freya—grant power to my spell tonight. Let my web attract men to be caught in its strands. Fill my life with men who think I am the best they've ever seen.*

Take the thread and, starting at the center, start to make the shape of a spiral—clockwise—adding beads at regular intervals. **Say:**

Each bead a fly
   Each bead a man
I'll capture them fast
   While I can

All shall come
   And none shall leave
Enchanted by this
   web I weave

This is my will
   So mote it be
This is my will
   So mote it be.

Once the web is finished, spend a few minutes strongly visualizing yourself in a social setting at the middle of an invisible web, surrounded by a number of men who are obviously interested in you. Then, without dropping any of the beads, carefully wrap the thread in some red velvet, add a drop of patchouli essential oil and either carry it with you to the next party or put it in a place of safekeeping.

CHECKLIST

Best to use: On a Friday evening during the waxing moon (the time of Venus, goddess of love).

How often: You probably won't need to use this any more than once every six months.

You will need:
A spool of red cotton thread
A tape measure
Beads
2 red candles
A little red velvet
Patchouli essential oil

Q: Is there a way I can dream of my ideal man?

A: **Yes, there is,** or even if you do not dream of an actual person, you should be able to have visions of things that will point you in the right direction. A good dream dictionary will help you to interpret these visions.

On the night of a full moon, when the sky is cloudless, take a purple pouch, some lavender, mugwort, cinnamon, rose or jasmine essential oil, and a glass of red wine outside, to a position where you will be able to sit comfortably on the ground, facing the moon. Slowly fill the pouch with the herbs, finishing with a pinch of cinnamon and a few drops of essential oil. As you do this, **chant in a sing-song voice:**

In my dreams, my love I shall see
Let true visions come to me
Come to me
Come to me
Locked in sleep, I shall see thee.

Blow into the pouch three times, then close it up. Hold the glass of wine up to the full moon in a salutary gesture, **and say:**

Great moon goddess, I pray you to bless this spell and to bless my sleep
with mystic dreams. Show me the man who is meant for me or
give me signs so that I shall know how to recognize him. Lift the veil
from my soul tonight and bring me wisdom. Blessed be thee.

Pour a little wine onto the ground in front of you as a libation in honor of the moon goddess, then drink the rest yourself. Place the pouch under your pillow. Sweet dreams should then follow.

CHECKLIST

Best to use: On the night of a full moon, when there is a clear sky.
How often: You only need to make the pouch once but you can recharge it with the ritual every now and again if necessary.

You will need:

A lavender- or purple-colored pouch
Fresh lavender
Fresh mugwort
Cinnamon powder
Rose or jasmine essential oils
Your favorite red wine

Q: How do I know if a man is worth going after or if I'll be *wasting my time?*

A. **There is nothing more frustrating** than putting all that effort into getting a man only to find out that he is a complete waste of time. Luckily, you can get a good idea about whether or not he is good enough for you by consulting the fates. This dice oracle will help to give the answers you seek. Then you will be able to decide whether to get a special new hairdo or stay in and watch your favorite TV show by the fire.

Cut out a 10 inch (25 cm) square of red velvet. Set the square upon a table and place a lit red candle behind it. Hold two dice in your hands and frame the question you wish to ask in your mind. For example, "Will I have anything in common with this man?" Concentrate hard on the question, then **say:**

Spirit guides, I call upon you this hour
to give me the truthful answer to the question I ask.
Be my counsel,
steer the dice and tell me what I need to know.

CHECKLIST

Best to use: Whenever you need some spiritual advice about a new man.

How often: Do not overuse this oracle, as the spirits, like your friends, will get tired of answering the same questions over and over again. In fact, use it too much and you will start to get silly answers.

You will need:
Some red velvet
A red candle
2 6-sided dice

Two	Opposites attract.
Three	This relationship may take some work to succeed.
Four	Friendship will always be important to both of you and love will grow from this.
Five	Beware; there may be troubles in this relationship.
Six	He will be caring and compassionate.
Seven	The number of Venus, this man will be passionate and sexy.
Eight	He may seem boring but he is reliable.
Nine	He may be a bit of a mystery at times. He may also be moody.
Ten	Karma. This is meant to be.
Eleven	Destiny is a mysterious thing. You are meant to discover the answer for yourself.
Twelve	This relationship may stifle the both of you because it seems so conventional.

Once you have asked the question and received the answer, remember to thank your spirit guides for their help. Although the number associations are based on ancient numerological wisdom, you may have different personal meanings for particular numbers. If this is so, it is fine to use those instead of the ones above, as your spirit guides will work better with ones you are familiar with.

Q: The man I want is seeing someone else. What can I do about it?

A: **Whether he is a new interest** or an ex you haven't gotten over yet, the plain fact is that you want to be with him, but someone else is coming between you. Ethically, magic should never be used to harm or to influence someone against their will, so using spells to do so is verging on the side of a darker kind of magic.

However, without affecting your karma, it is possible to open up the lines of connection between you both, open up his eyes to the relationship he is in, so that he will be able to see whether it is right for him or not, and then leave it to the universe to sort out. That way, if the two of them are not destined to be together, they will split up, and if the two of you are really soul mates, he will find his way to you. But if they are really meant to be together, this spell will not work and you will be better off addressing your feelings, maybe with one of the spells in the Dumpsville chapter.

At full moon, set three white candles on an altar. Place one candle to represent him in the middle, one for the other woman on his left, and one

for you on his right. Tie a brown ribbon around his candle, a blue one around hers, and a green around yours. Rub each candle with almond oil from the base to the wick, while visualizing the person and saying their name. Tie the ends of the brown ribbon to one end of the green and the blue. **Then say:**

He to me, he to she
She wants he, let him see
Open his eyes, open his heart
If it is to be, let them part
Then he to me shall loving turn

As these magic candles burn
And love shall flower between
he and me
So be it, if it is meant to be.

Now untie the ribbon ends, giving him "free will" to choose, and sit quietly in contemplation for a while before lighting the candles and allowing them to burn down to stumps.

CHECKLIST

Best to use: On the night of a full moon.

How often: It is only necessary to do this once. If it doesn't work then maybe fate is trying to tell you something.

You will need:
Almond oil
3 white candles in holders
A brown, a blue, and a green
   ribbon

Q: How can I attract a rich guy?

A: **Of course, you should love a guy** for who he is, not how much moola he has in his pocket. Right? Well, we are only human and it would be nice to sometimes date a Mr. Wonderful who doesn't count every last penny. After all, diamonds are a girl's best friend.

Perform this ritual outside on the night of the full moon. Mark a large circle on the ground with something non-permanent, such as salt. Ascertain where north, south, east, and west are and place a green candle at each point. When you are ready, place a net bag, some coins, a plastic male figurine, a model car, and some silk underwear in the circle and light the candles. Place the bag in the north and the figurine, car, and coins at the other directional points.

Sit quietly in the center of the circle for a few moments, then stand and pick up the bag. Traveling in a clockwise direction (deosil), walk around the circle, picking up the objects and placing them in the bag. **Say:**

I shall hunt and I shall catch
I shall stalk and I shall snatch
Bring me a man with plenty of cash.

Once you have your "booty" in the bag, walk around the circle clockwise (deosil) again, this time starting in the east and finishing in the north. At each quarter, kneel before the candle and **say the following prayer:**

Powers of the [insert name of direction] hear my request
 And help me in my magic quest
A man of money to fall for me
 As I do will, so shall it be.

At the end of the ritual, wrap the bag in the silk underwear. Blow out the candles and clear the ground so that no trace of your spell making exists. Place the bag wrapped in the underwear near to where you keep your checkbook. Then go out and party!

CHECKLIST

Best to use: On the night of a full moon, outside and in good weather.

How often: It is best to only use this spell once every few months.

You will need:

Salt
A compass
4 green candles
A net bag
Coins, of various denominations
A plastic male figurine, from a toy store
A model car; a Ferrari would be quite appropriate
Silk underwear

Q: How can I make sure the first date goes off with a bang?

A. **Well, you don't really want an** out-of-control explosion, do you? But a little fizzle and sizzle on a first date is always a good start. Remember, first impressions really do count, so make sure you're dressed to the nines and perhaps perform one of the Sexy Seductress Makeovers from the first chapter. However, this talisman will really make sure your date is a magical experience!

Fold a sheet of plain cardboard in half. With a red pen, draw a heart shape, small enough to fit into your purse or pocket, so that one edge lies along the fold. Cut out the doubled-up heart. It should now look a little like a greeting card. On the inside, draw two more hearts, linked together, with the red pen. Inside each heart, write his name and yours. You may wish to add other decorations that symbolize the date to you as well. When this is done, lay the card on the ground beneath a red candle. Light the candle and walk around it three times in a clockwise direction. As you do so, **say this chant:**

*When my lover looks at me
He shall like all that he sees
Heart shall leap and heart shall bound
He shall think that love is found
By this talisman I do will
This date my every wish to fill.*

Blow out the candle and let a little of the melted wax fall onto your cardboard talisman, sealing it. When the wax has cooled, place the talisman in your purse or a pocket of the outfit you will wear for the date. He will not be able to resist your charms.

CHECKLIST

Best to use: A few hours or the night before your first date.
How often: Only when you are about to go on your first date— don't repeat it for subsequent dates, as its magic should still be sufficient.

You will need:
A red pen
A red candle
A sheet of plain cardboard

Under your spell

*You've found a fantastic guy, there are just
a few little, niggly things that are not quite right.
This is usually where the first arguments begin,
so make it easy on yourself with a bit of magical
maneuvering. Whether he's lousy at calling you
or you want to make sure he has eyes for no one
but your beautiful self, use these spells to help
train him to please you. You may even decide that
you want him to commit to you—forever!
Whatever magic you choose to try, you'll soon
have the perfect relationship that will make all
your friends green with envy.*

Q: How can I get him to call me?

A: **There is nothing worse than** sitting by the phone waiting for him to call. You can sit there for hours, not really able to concentrate on anything else. Then it rings, you pounce to pick it up, and find that it's only your great-aunt Flo. When it comes to communication, men can be frustrating creatures. Generally, they don't have the need to make contact like we girls do, so they can't understand why we need to hear from them so often. However, here's a way to save yourself some waiting time. Try this spell and he'll be dialing your number before he even knows it.

Sit quietly and light your favorite incense. With a needle, carve an upward-pointing arrow into the wax of a silver candle. Then write your name and telephone number on some white cardboard. Place the candle on top of the cardboard and light it. **Now sit back and chant the following:**

[Insert his name], hear my will
I am in your heart
I am in your mind
I am in your thoughts
You need to call me
You want to call me
You will call me.

Repeat the chant nine times, then concentrate on his face in your mind for as long as you can. If you can manage 30 minutes of thinking about him, so much the better, as the power you generate through your will becomes much more concentrated over a longer period. Your thought waves should then reach him and he will feel an urgent need to talk to you.

CHECKLIST

Best to use: Whenever you need him to call you, but all the better on a Wednesday.

How often: As often as you need.

You will need:

Your favorite incense stick and an incense stick holder

A needle

A silver-colored candle

White cardboard

A pen

Q: How do I know if he's cheating on me?

A: **Insecurity** should play only a small and fairly insignificant part in any relationship. However, if the worry that your beloved is cheating is taking over your every thought, then that insecurity is a big problem. Maybe you are noticing little signs that have made you uneasy, or perhaps there has been a change in his attitude toward you. Whatever the cause, the best solution is to tackle it and find out the truth. If you cannot get a direct answer from your man's lips, try this candle oracle. However, you will also need to ask yourself a tough question: If the relationship is causing you this much pain, is it even worth carrying on with it?

Set up a small altar where you can safely position a white, a black, and a gray candle. You need to be sure there are no drafts in the room. Pour a drop of cardamom essential oil onto a tissue and rub it into the white candle in an upward direction. **As you do so, say:**

Candle of white, you are true. If he be faithful, let it be you
That burns the brightest but stays until last
To show his love shall hold fast.

Now rub the oil into the black candle, **saying:**

Candle of black, you are true. If he be a cheat, let it be you
That burns the brightest and longest shall be
To show him faithless unto me.

Finally, rub the oil into the gray candle, **saying:**

Candle of gray, you are true. If there is no straight answer, let it be you
That burns the brightest and longest to show
Other problems in this relationship grow.

Place all three candles on the altar with your beloved's picture behind and light them all as quickly as possible. Let the candles burn down, and the one that burns the longest will give you your answer. If it is the gray candle, this may mean that other problems are causing you to pick up those little disquieting signs, in which case you may want to try the method of divination featured on the next page.

CHECKLIST

Best to use: On the night of a full moon.

How often: Do not overuse this spell. Once every six months, if necessary, is enough.

You will need:
A white, a black, and a gray candle
A photograph or a drawing of
 your beloved
Cardamom essential oil

Q: Is there a way of finding answers to my relationship questions?

A: **No one has all the answers** to what is happening in their lives. This can sometimes leave you feeling out of control and unsure of which direction to turn next. This is especially true in relationships, and it is no coincidence that the most commonly asked questions to clairvoyants and card readers at psychic fairs are about love. But if you can tune yourself into the psychic tides through your subconscious, you can gain the answers for yourself, through the ancient art of dowsing.

Light a white candle and your favorite incense. These are not strictly necessary, but I find they help to calm and focus the mind for the task ahead. If you do not have a dowsing pendulum, simply loop some thread through a ring and knot it so that the makeshift pendulum is about 6-7 inches (15-18 cm) long. Hold the thread of either pendulum at the top and let it hang freely.

Begin by asking the pendulum some simple yes/no questions that you already know the answer to. After a short while you should feel the weight of the pendulum move and notice it swing either clockwise or counterclockwise. It may also oscillate, and the strength of movement will also vary. From the questions you have asked you should be able to discern which way it moves for yes and how it moves for no, or no answer.

At this point you are ready to begin asking the serious questions. Sit quietly and focus on your question. Let the pendulum hang and swing the way it wants to. It is very important to keep all other thoughts out of your head, since they could influence the way the pendulum swings. If you are unsure of an answer, try asking it again, to see if the pendulum still reacts in the same way.

CHECKLIST

Best to use: Anytime you need answers.

How often: Try not to use it more than once a day.

You will need:

A white candle

Your favorite incense stick and an incense stick holder

A dowsing pendulum, or a piece of thread and a favorite ring

?Q: How can I keep him faithful?

A. **Some men believe it is a** necessary part of their male instinct to sow as many wild oats as possible. However, if you are in an exclusive relationship and truly in love, this should never be an issue. Just in case he needs reminding, however, that the grass isn't greener on the other side, here is a charm to bind him to your side and to your heart.

Light a green candle, then place some caraway seeds in a green pouch—in herbal lore these seeds are said to have the power to make a lover remain faithful. Add a lock of his hair or his nail clippings and close up the pouch. Wrap the gold-colored ribbon around the pouch and tie in seven knots. As you do this, **say:**

[Insert his name], I name you as my love.
With this spell I bind you close to my heart,
that you shall never stray. With this spell I bind
your eyes, that they shall be attracted only to m
With this spell I bind your lips that you speak
words of seduction only to me. And with this spell
I bind your body that you shall desire only m
All this I do will until I say otherwise.
By sun and by moon, by night and day,
as I do will so shall it be.

Hide the pouch somewhere where your man either sits (such as under the sofa) or sleeps (under the mattress), or failing that just ensure that it is placed away from prying eyes.

CHECKLIST

Best done: On a Friday, at midnight, as near to a full moon as possible.

How often: Once is usually enough.

You will need:

A green candle
Caraway seeds
A green pouch
A lock of his hair or his nail clippings
A gold-colored ribbon

Q: Can I make my vacation romance last?

A: **Vacation romances have a horrible habit** of fizzling out once the last postcards have arrived home. Even so, there are couples who have met on vacation and spent the rest of their lives together. If this is how you'd like it to be, try this bit of magic to keep the sun shining on your relationship.

Light two red candles and a rose incense stick. Place a photograph of you both, some "Everlasting" flower seeds, and an object he has had contact with on a red washcloth. Gather the edges together and tie at the top with red ribbon. Holding the bag against your heart, visualize the two of you together, your hearts joined by a stream of golden light. **Say:**

> *I conjure our love as a golden glow*
> *Stronger between us shall it grow*
> *By bud and stem, by leaf and flower,*
> *It shall grow deeper by this power.*
> *By root and seed, I call to thee*
> *And soon together we'll always be.*
> *Although the vacation is over,*
> *You shall always be my lover*
> *As I do will, so shall it be.*

Now it is time to plant the rosebush in your garden, but put the washcloth in the hole so that it sits underneath the bush. Fill the earth back in and firm it down, then give the new bush a good watering while visualizing it glowing with the golden light you saw between your hearts. Now take great care to look after the rose—a dead plant will mean a dead spell.

CHECKLIST

Best to use: When the moon is waxing as soon after you return from vacation as possible.

How often: Just once.

You will need:

2 red candles

A rose incense stick and an incense stick holder

A photograph of both of you together

Something that the man in question has had contact with, such as hair, sand, or soil

"Everlasting" flower seeds (Latin name: *Helichrysum*; other common name: strawflower)

A red washcloth

A red ribbon

A newly bought rosebush

Q: What can I do to make him commit?

A: So you've been with your guy for ages and you're convinced it's a match made in heaven. You want him to commit to you for good, however, he seems oblivious to your desires. Obviously you feel that you've waited long enough, so maybe it's time to use a little magical persuasion to speed things along. Use this spell and you'll soon be walking up the aisle.

Sitting under the light of the full moon, take a garter and sew onto it all those symbolic wedding decorations, including a ring. Spread them around the garter's circumference so that they are equidistant to each other. When you have finished, sprinkle the charm with rose water and **say:**

Moon goddess, queen of heaven
Bless this charm I make tonight.
Lend your power unto the spell
Enchant it with your holy light.
May my deepest wish be granted

A wedded woman I would be.
May this magic garter charm my love
That he soon asks to marry me.
Within a year a bride I'll be,
And it harm none, so shall it be.

Kiss the garter three times and leave it somewhere where it can soak up the power of the moon's energies overnight. At dawn the next morning, retrieve the garter and, if possible, wrap it in a piece of clothing your beloved will be wearing in the next day or so (but remember to remove it before he does).

Alternatively, leave the charm somewhere where its power will be felt, such as under the bed or behind a piece of furniture. But wherever it is placed, the important thing is that your man doesn't find it; not only will the magic be dissipated, but you will also have a lot of explaining to do.

CHECKLIST

Best done: On the night of a full moon, with a clear sky.

How often: Just once.

You will need:

A garter, homemade or bought
Small wedding decorations, such as lucky horseshoes
A small ring or a brass curtain ring
Needle and thread
Rose water

?Q: How can I ensure a romantic vacation with my man?

A: **You want romantic** beaches and candlelit dinners, while all he wants from a vacation is a few rounds of golf. Unfortunately, the golf usually wins. To ensure that this year he takes you on a vacation you'll want to remember forever—for all the right reasons—make this talisman to turn his mind to those far-off, exotic places full of sun, sea, and seduction.

Place two sheets of white cardboard together and draw an octagon on one of them with a red pen. Keeping both pieces together, cut around the shape. Next, cut out small pictures from a vacation brochure that you feel are appropriate to your wishes. Place the pictures between the two pieces of cardboard and glue the cards together at the edges, so that the pictures are inside. With the red pen, draw a sun symbol—a small circle with a dot at the center—in the middle of one of the pieces of cardboard. From this circle, draw eight arrows, facing outward, equidistantly spaced around the octagon. Repeat on the other side of the cardboard package. Light a white candle and an incense stick. Pass the talisman over the candle and **say**:

Power of fire, bless this charm, that it encourages [insert his name] to wish for the same vacation that I desire.

Pass the talisman through the incense smoke and repeat the above blessing, replacing "fire" with "air." Sprinkle the talisman with water, again repeating the charm and invoking the power of the water element, then sprinkle it with earth, amending the blessing to represent the power of the earth element. Once the talisman has been consecrated, leave it discreetly in a room that you both spend a lot of time in. It is also a good idea to leave vacation brochures in the same room too, so that he really gets the hint.

?Q: What can I do to make him more affectionate?

A: **Some men have great difficulty** showing their true feelings, often hiding them under a mask of indifference or humor. If you are someone who thrives on displays of affection, this can be difficult. Instead of sulking when he doesn't tell you how much he loves you, turn your mind to changing the way he relates to you. This magic should help him discard the shell he has built up around himself and encourage him to share his innermost feelings with you.

Light a pink candle and a rose incense stick. Take a large white feather and use the quill end to write your lover's name on one side of a bar of soap. On the other side of the soap, inscribe a heart. Hold the soap over the candle flame, making sure to hold it high enough not to melt the soap or burn your fingers, and **say:**

By fire's great passion
By fire's warmth
Open up [insert his name]'s heart to me.

Now hold the soap in the incense smoke and **say:**

By air that brings freedom
By the breath of life
Blow away the cage around
his heart.

CHECKLIST

Best to use: During the waxing moon and when you are close to the ocean.
How often: Once in a while, when needed.

You will need:
A pink candle
A rose incense stick and an
   incense stick holder
A large white bird's feather
A small bar of soap
A bowl of earth
An item of his clothing

Sprinkle a little earth over the soap and **say:**

> *By Mother Earth who nurtures us,*
> *Who supports us in life and receives us in death,*
> *Steady his trust and steady his love.*

Now wrap the soap in an item of his clothing and take it to the edge of the ocean at high tide. Unwrap it and hold it close to your heart, **saying:**

> *Ever flowing waters, timeless seas,*
> *I ask you to soften [insert his name]'s feelings.*
> *And as this soap melts, so shall his heart melt toward me*
> *To open up and to show me love.*
> *So be it.*

Throw the bar of soap into the waves and walk away without looking back.

Red hot
seduction

Every girl wants to be a babe in the bedroom and ensure her guy always remembers her with a smile on his face! Whether you wish to enhance your own pleasure or bring him to his knees, all you have to do is work a little bit of magic between the sheets. So spice up your love life by getting your wand out. These sexy spells will turn you into a red-hot seductive siren and him into your love slave.

Q: How can I be a goddess in the bedroom?

A: **Whatever happens between** you and your man in the future, it's only natural that you'd want him to remember you as the best lover he ever had. To guarantee this, add a little supernatural boost to the skills you already have—naturally—and make sure he looks upon you with awe.

Before you start the ritual, take a long, hot, scented bath to prepare yourself to become an earth-bound love goddess. Set up a small altar in a room with a full-length mirror and stereo equipment. It is best to do this ritual naked, although, if you prefer, you can wear your favorite, sexiest clothing. Light two red candles and a patchouli or jasmine incense stick. Take three lengths of red chiffon and tie them together at one end. Braid the remaining chiffon lengths and tie the other ends together. Take some ylang ylang essential oil and anoint the braid at both ends and in the middle. **Recite:**

I charge this sash with the power of desire and the energy of Eros. With its magic I call down upon me the powers of the goddess of love.

Tie the sash around your waist so that it hangs loosely about your hips. Then take a glass of red wine and hold it above your head while **toasting the goddess:**

Ancient triple goddess,
on you I call
Maiden, mother, and crone
I ask for your blessing
I ask for your knowledge.
In your aspect as goddess of
love and desire
I ask that you grant me
your power
That any man who visits my bed
Shall think me the queen of love.
Blessed be.

Drink some of the wine. Put on your favorite, seductive music and begin to dance sexily in front of the mirror. See your new sexual power surrounding you like an aura. To end the ritual, thank the goddess in your own words. When your lover next comes to call, either wear the sash or drape it decoratively over the bed.

CHECKLIST

Best to use: On a Friday as close as possible to a full moon.
How often: As often as you like, although you will need to make up the chiffon braid only once.

You will need:
A full-length mirror
Your favorite sexy music and a stereo
2 red candles
A patchouli or jasmine incense stick
   and an incense stick holder
3 6-foot (1.8 m) lengths of red chiffon
Ylang ylang essential oil
A glass of red wine

?Q: How can I get him to fulfill my every desire?

A: **As is often commented on,** men seem to come from an entirely different planet than women. They speak a different language—or at least they don't understand ours. This means they have a tendency to be completely unaware of our wants and needs, no matter how many hints we drop. To help him understand the subtleties of female vocabulary and make him sensitive to your feelings, use this simple spell. He'll soon be granting your every wish.

Take a seashell and write his name on it three times with a red pen. As you do this, visualize him picking up the shell, which represents your energy, placing it to his ear, and listening. Wrap the shell in an unwashed piece of his clothing and fasten the whole package with a silver ribbon—because silver is the color of Mercury and symbolic of communication. Hold the package in front of you and **say:**

Mars shall take Venus's hand
And at last shall understand
What it is she has to say
And will want to please
her in every way.

By Mercury's help and
Mercury's spell
Everything shall turn out well.
Mars shall grant her every desire
And of her wishes he'll never tire.

CHECKLIST
Best to use: On a Wednesday, during the waxing moon.
How often: You shouldn't need to repeat this spell too often.

You will need:
A small seashell
A red pen
A small, unwashed garment belonging to the man in question
A silver ribbon

Place the package under the bed for seven days and nights to allow the energy to work upon him. After this, bury the shell and ribbon in the garden, and wash his clothing, before he wonders where it's been! He should now be more in tune with the way you communicate and will know exactly what you want.

WARNING: SUPERSTRONG SPELL—USE WITH CARE

HAS IT WORKED?

If he is acting like a faithful puppy waiting to please you, then yes!

A word of caution: Be sure you really want this level of attention. Some women might find this a bit boring after a while.

Q: How can I make him my love slave?

A: **Does he come to your place,** throw himself on the sofa, and spend his time watching sports when you'd rather he was lavishing all his attention on you? Or could you dress up in the sexiest bustier you possess, do the dance of the seven veils in front of him, and find he still pays you no attention? Maybe that is exaggerating it a bit, but if you feel that your man isn't giving you the loving attention in the bedroom that you deserve, perform this simple ritual and you'll soon have him eating out of your hand on demand.

Do this ritual while bathed in the light of the full moon. Place rose petals and seven vanilla beans—symbols of love and seduction—into a copper dish and stir clockwise with your finger three times, **while reciting:**

Scents of love
Moon's power above
Make my man
A slave to love.

This golden chain
His neck attire
He shall obey
My every desire.

Lay a man's gold neck chain on top of the rose petals and then place a red silk square over the dish. Leave the bowl and its contents to absorb the moon's rays, which have been given some lust energy by the red of the silk. During the next day place the bowl and its contents in a dark place. The next evening, invite your lover around for a sumptuous meal. After your feast, present him with the gold chain and he'll do your every bidding.

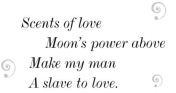

CHECKLIST
Best to use: On a Friday night at the full moon.
How often: You'll probably need to do this only once for every lover.

You will need:
Rose petals
7 vanilla beans
A copper dish
A man's gold neck chain
A red silk square

Q: Can I stop him from falling asleep right away?

A: **It's so frustrating,** isn't it? After great sex you want an intimate, loving cuddle and a chat, but instead you get a turned back and almost immediate snoring. You could try kicking him awake, but it's not very romantic and he won't be happy about the bruises. So instead, why don't you try this herbal potion, full of plants that are reputed to keep the mind fresh and active?

Lay a white handkerchief in front of you on the floor. Make sure it is clean and new for the purpose of the spell. Place a red stone in the center of the handkerchief—red is the color of energy so its vibrations should help keep him awake. Place a single drop of patchouli essential oil on one corner of the handkerchief. Then put a drop of peppermint essential oil on the next corner, basil essential oil on the next corner, and lemon essential oil on the last corner. Gather up the edges of the handkerchief and tie the pouch together with red ribbon. Now stand up and shake the bag, feeling the stone move as you do so. **Repeat the following:**

This charm I shall shake
To keep you awake
Your company to keep
To not lose you in sleep.
Touching and sharing
Kisses and caring
Until at the last
We BOTH shall sleep fast.

Place the charm under the mattress, on his side of the bed, and look forward to a little caring consideration after making love.

Q: Can sex magic improve other areas of my life?

A: **Sex magic and magical sex** are often associated with the ancient Eastern belief system of tantra. In fact, tantra encompasses more than mystical beliefs, such as the principles of meditation, yoga, and ritual, and it is a term that is often misunderstood. Nevertheless, tantric sexual practices have had much to teach the West about the power and beauty of sexual energy. Here is a small and simple ritual adapted from Eastern wisdom that can be used to improve your life through harnessing the power of your own sexuality. However, as it is a ritual done in the spirit of love and sharing, do not use its power for anything selfish or abusive.

Mix one drop of frankincense essential oil with two teaspoons of almond oil and put aside for later. Before your night of pleasure, prepare yourself by taking a long, dreamy, candlelit bath full of your favorite scent. Spend your soaking time visualizing what it is that you want to achieve. Upon getting out, wrap yourself in a bathrobe until dry. Place a dab of the frankincense and almond oil on your finger and anoint your body in the following three places: the third eye; over the heart; and just below your navel. As you do so, **affirm the following:**

> *I anoint myself for this magical rite*
> *The power I shall raise this night*
> *Is for the purpose of [state your purpose].*
> *So shall it be*
> *So shall it be*
> *So shall it be.*

Just before making love—either with a partner or yourself—light a red candle. Remember that the sexual act should be loving and not rushed; it

is not merely the means to an end. At the point of orgasm, visualize your needs again strongly—I admit, this may take a little practice—and imagine all of your released energy taking your wish out into the universe. Afterward, do not dwell on what you have asked for; just let it go and see what happens.

CHECKLIST
Best to use: When you have a particular, important goal in mind, or for healing or helping others.
How often: Not too often—this can be a very powerful form of magic and should not be overused.

You will need:
Frankincense essential oil
Almond oil
A loving and willing sexual partner (optional)
A red candle

Q: Is there a magical charm that will enhance my pleasure in bed?

A: Everyone wants to have a toe-tinglingly memorable experience whenever they make love. And you are no different. When you are elderly and in a rocking chair, you want people to wonder why you have that big smile on your face. If only they could see what you were remembering! Of course a lot of the chemistry comes down to who you're with, but if you want to give your lovemaking a boost, mix up this sensuously magical potion full of essential oils that practically reek of sexual pleasure.

Mix four teaspoons of rose water with two drops each of rosewood, neroli, and ylang ylang or jasmine essential oils in a spray bottle. Stir the oils vigorously in a clockwise direction, which brings in positive energies, until they are evenly dispersed. As you do so, **chant the following:**

Flowers of love
Powers of love
Bring me desire
Bring me pleasure
Bring me a night I'll remember
For all my living years.

Place the top on the spray bottle, then spray the mixture over the bed sheets, **saying as you do so:**

CHECKLIST
Best to use: Just before you intend to make love.
How often: As often as you like.

You will need:
Rose water
Rosewood, neroli, and ylang ylang
  or jasmine essential oils
A spray bottle

I bless this bed with a thousand
pleasures
A thousand skillful caresses
And an eternity of love
So shall it be.

When you make love, you will be surrounded with the powerful sensual energies of these flowers, as well as the lovely scent.

WARNING: SUPERSTRONG SPELL—USE WITH CARE

HAS IT WORKED?

If your love life has become the stuff of legend, then obviously the spell has worked!

A word of caution: Make sure this spell doesn't make you burn out with passion—remember, everything in moderation!

Q: How can I make him last longer in bed?

A: **When you have** spent time dolling yourself up to look seductive, and used all your best techniques on him, it is especially frustrating to have your man last just five minutes before lapsing into a snoring slumber. You want a marathon runner, not a sprinter! You need to increase his endurance and staying power. This is one of those cases when a bit of sympathetic magic is called for—and no, that doesn't mean a cup of coffee and a meaningful chat.

To begin with, take some air-drying clay and fashion it into a small manikin to resemble your beloved. Press his hair or nail clippings into the clay as you do so, to impart his essence into the spell. I will leave it up to your artistic ability and imagination as to how you fashion his manhood!

Let the clay dry thoroughly. With a mortar and pestle mix together some ocher, powdered ginseng, and ground acorn, grinding them all to a fine powder. This is going to be used on the genitals, so mix as much as you need for that area of your manikin. Next, add a couple of drops of ginger essential oil and stir it in until it forms a thin paste, like paint. Apply the paste to the genitals of the figure while **saying:**

A little for him, a lot for me
I call upon the powers that be,
To increase his virility.
Make him last, make him strong,
Make my pleasure be all night long.

Let the paint dry then wrap the figure in red velvet and keep it in a safe place in the bedroom, where it will not be disturbed. The power of this spell will wane quickly—in about 24 hours—so it may need to be refreshed every so often.

CHECKLIST

Best to use: When your lover needs an energy boost. The energies for this spell are at their greatest on a Tuesday near a new moon.

How often: Don't overdo it; after all, you don't want to wear him out completely, do you?

You will need:

Some air-drying clay

A lock of his hair or his nail clippings

A mortar and pestle

Ocher (powdered iron oxide) or powdered red paint

Powdered ginseng

Ground acorn

Ginger essential oil

Soft red velvet

Lies, guys, & goodbyes

Every relationship has its problems. Sometimes they can be easily solved with a little bit of extra communication, but other problems can bring true love to breaking point. Whether it's a question of lies, jealousy, bad habits, or simply not opening up, there's a spell here to pour oil on troubled waters. Even those pesky relatives who treat you as the girlfriend from hell can be tamed with a little bit of timely enchantment. So stop your suffering now and magic your way into "happy ever after."

?Q: How can I curb his possessiveness?

A: **Are you starting to feel** like a prisoner in your relationship? Does he watch everything you do? Check your e-mails and messages and accuse you of going behind his back? It doesn't take much to tell you that this is an unhealthy position for any relationship to be in. There cannot be true love between two people unless there is also trust. If your man doesn't trust you, try using this spell to dampen his jealousy. If, however, his feelings are too strong to be controlled even by magic, then maybe you should reconsider whether he is the right one for you. And it goes without saying that if his possessiveness shows a violent streak, bail out immediately.

Find a quiet time and place to perform this spell, so that you won't be disturbed. Tie three green cotton threads together at one end. Wrap the threads around a white candle and secure them at the other end with another knot. Hold the candle to your third eye, in the middle of your forehead, and bring to mind examples of your partner's possessiveness. Then untie the knot at the bottom and slowly begin to unwind the strands, **saying as you do so:**

With your heart, don't hold so tight, let me wander from your sight.
Without fear that I will stray, meet someone else, or go away.
Trust me when I'm not around, with these words you are bound.

Now spend some time visualizing him as a changed person, trusting you whatever you decide to do and wherever you go. Next, place the threads in a fireproof dish, away from anything flammable, and light the candle, **saying:**

With this flame, I claim freedom from his possessiveness.

Use the candle to set light to the threads. As they catch fire, **recite:**

Burn these binding threads of distrust
  Into trusting and unconditional love between him and me.
    So be it.

When the ash of the threads has cooled, sprinkle it on the garden and plant some pretty flowers in it.

CHECKLIST

Best to use: On a Saturday during a waning moon.

How often: Just once should be sufficient. If you feel the need to do it more than once then this guy is not "the one."

You will need:

3 green cotton threads
A white candle
A fireproof dish

Q: Is there a magical way for me to deal with my own jealousy?

A. **The green-eyed monster of jealousy** has caused many a relationship breakup. It is understandable enough: you have the most fantastic boyfriend in the world and you are afraid of losing him to somebody else. However, your possessiveness will soon drive him crazy—in all the wrong ways—and will probably push him away. So, if jealousy is your shortcoming, act now to stamp it out and save yourself a lot of unnecessary pain.

Light a white candle and place a smooth, black, palm-sized pebble in a bowl of salt water. Salt water acts to take away negativity, leaving, as it were, a clean slate. **Repeat the following:**

I cleanse you of all previous influences.

Sit for a while and meditate on what makes you jealous and why. Are there any specific circumstances? Could it be a lack of self-esteem on your part? Is he always flirting with others? Knowing what presses your buttons will allow you to devise a strategy for dealing with it in the practical world, while the magic in this spell will help you cope with it on an inner level. Feel how your jealousy hurts you and understand that such pain is not good for you. Promise yourself that whenever you feel jealous, you will silently repeat the **following affirmation:**

CHECKLIST
Best to use: On a Saturday during a waning moon.
How often: Once for each relationship.

You will need:
A white candle
A smooth, black, palm-sized pebble
A bowl of salt water

I am a worthwhile and beautiful person. Everything will be well.

Take the pebble from the water and hold it in your hands as it dries. Mentally "make friends" with it and ask it to absorb all your negative feelings of possessiveness as they arise. From now on, carry it with you like a protective talisman. When you instinctively feel it is full of bad vibes, give it another cleansing by lighting a white candle, placing it in a bowl of salt water, and visualizing all of the jealousy being washed away. At the end of the ritual, pour the jealousy-ridden water down the drain, where it belongs.

Q: How can I stop jealous gossip before it ruins our relationship?

A. **You think he's the most** wonderful guy in the world. Unfortunately, so do many others, and they'll stop at nothing to take him from you, including spreading malicious gossip designed to split you up. It's time to fight back, but instead of using your fists, use a little binding spell. It won't cause anyone any harm, but it should make them think twice before they open their mouths to disrespect you again.

Using a needle, carve the name of the troublemaker (or all of them if there are more than one) into the wax of a black candle. Place the candle on an altar and sprinkle salt around it in a circle. Light the candle, visualize the person or persons who are causing you so many problems, and **say:**

All those that seek to cause me ill
Bend you now unto my will.
Lips that talk of me are sealed
And all hurts gone before are healed.
No more shall your malice cause me pain
My hurt shall no more be your gain.
Thus this spell your tongue shall bind
Unless your heart and words be kind.

Let the candle burn down to a stump, then place it and the salt in a black pouch. Bury the pouch in the garden and place a large stone over the top.

CHECKLIST

Best to use: When you know who is causing the trouble and it is getting to be more than you can bear.

Do this spell during a waning moon.

How often: No more than once every few months.

Q: How can I make him open up more?

A: **The art of communication** is not always a strong point with many men, especially when it comes to discussing their emotions. It just isn't "manly." If this is the case with your man, it could cause problems with your relationship, especially if he will not tell you how he feels or what he wants. Of course, you can't force him to talk, and if you try he will probably run for the hills. Most men need time and trust before they will open up, but this healing visualization exercise will help build that bond between you more quickly.

Sit on a comfortable cushion in a quiet place where you won't be disturbed. Light a dark blue candle and some rose incense. Close your eyes and slow your breathing until you feel relaxed. On the in-breath, imagine roots growing from the base of your spine and connecting you to Mother Earth. On every subsequent in-breath, imagine a golden light flowing through the roots and filling your body. At the same time, imagine a beam of golden light entering the top of your head, filling you with healing energy. On each out-breath, let go of any stress or anxieties you may be carrying.

Keep breathing deeply while moving some of the golden energy to your heart chakra. Feel it expand with love. Now, visualize your man sitting opposite you and send the golden light from your heart to his with loving, healing wishes. See the energy rise from his heart and into his throat chakra, turning a rich dark blue as it does. Sending healing energy to the throat chakra will help him express himself better. **Say:**

I send you blessings to heal your heart.
Open it up.
Be no longer afraid.
This love is unconditionally yours.

When you withdraw your energy from him, do so slowly and carefully.
Practice this every night for at least a week.

CHECKLIST

Best to use: On a Wednesday evening during the waning moon.
How often: As often as you feel is necessary.

You will need:
A dark blue candle
A rose incense stick and
   an incense stick holder
A comfortable cushion

Q: How can I make his family and friends like me?

A: So, his family or friends have taken a dislike to you even though, as far as you know, you have never done anything to upset them. Maybe they just don't think you're good enough for him—and no one ever will be—or perhaps they are jealous that he is spending more time with you than with them. Either way, you've become the unwilling and undeserving target of their enmity. There's certainly no point in making the situation worse by retaliating, so why not use magic instead, to open their hearts to your wonderful nature?

Draw a large circle on a 6 inch (15 cm) square of cardboard, then draw a small circle at the center. For as many people as you want to like you, draw lines from the center to the edge of the circle at equidistant points. Write a person's name on every line and write your name in the center circle. Look over some polished tumbled gemstones and pick one that you feel represents you. Place it in the center of the circle. Choose other stones to represent the other people, and name each one by holding it and visualizing the person you are naming it for. Then place the stone on the appropriate spoke of the circle. Light a pink candle and spend some time visualizing each gemstone as the person it symbolizes. **Say:**

> *Come closer and feel the warmth of my heart*
> *Come closer and see the friendship in my eyes*
> *Come closer and know me*
> *Come closer and like me.*

Move each stone about ¼ inch (0.5 cm) along its spoke toward the center, while seeing yourself in a happy situation together with these people. Every night light the candle, repeat the chant, and move the stones inward a little more, until they all meet in the center. At this point put all the stones

together in a pouch or wrap them in a piece of tissue paper
and carry them with you whenever you are meeting his friends or family
and until you feel them warming up to you.

CHECKLIST

Best to use: On a Tuesday
evening close to the new moon.
How often: You may need
to repeat this spell a couple of
times for particularly stubborn
individuals.

You will need:
A 6 inch (15 cm) square
  of cardboard
A pen
A tumbled gemstone for each
  friend or relation and one
  for yourself
A pink candle
A pouch or sheet of tissue paper

Q: Can magic help me cope with unrequited love?

A. **You may have fallen head over heels** with someone, but that doesn't guarantee that they are going to feel the same way about you. It can be one of the most soul-destroying situations when you find that your love is unrequited; that the man you want more than anyone either doesn't want to know you or loves someone else. You may have tried every love spell in the book, and they haven't worked for the simple reason that it just isn't meant to be. This is no help, however, if your heart is breaking and your life is falling apart. Instead of using magic in a futile attempt to change destiny, use it to help yourself through the situation, so that you can regain your confidence and self-respect once more.

Find a suitable place to leave a glass jar and a pile of beans: the dressing table in your bedroom would be a good spot, if it isn't too cluttered. Every night and morning, place a bean in the jar while **chanting:**

The more I love me
The less I want thee.
I have come to accept
It wasn't to be.

As the beans grow
Each day I'll know
There'll be another at my door
Who'll deserve me more.

CHECKLIST

Best to use: As soon as you find yourself in the downward spiral of unrequited love, whatever the day or moon's phase. This is an emotional emergency!

How often: As often as you need this magical comfort.

You will need:
A glass jar
Some beans, broad beans are best, or beads

As you say this, imagine firmly shutting a door between yourself and this man, before you turn away to face a beautiful landscape of fields, flowers, and trees that represents your future. When the jar is full, if you still feel your healing isn't strong enough, empty out the beans and start again. In real life, try to physically distance yourself from this man—constant contact will only serve to reopen the wound. It may take a few weeks to complete this healing, because feelings of love contain a very strong energy.

Q: What can I do to make sure he doesn't lie to me?

A. **Do you suspect your guy** of lying to you? Perhaps he has lied in the past and you find it hard now to believe anything he says. As with any relationship problems that involve issues of trust, you must first ask yourself whether he really is worth all the pain you are currently going through. If you think he is, and it is worth trying a little magic to improve his credibility, try this spell.

Prepare a small altar space with a feather, some red ink, and a sheet of paper. Sit quietly and focus on your desired outcome. Then take the feather, dip it in the ink, and write his name on the paper three times. This may take a while and a lot of concentration, but that is fine since it will focus your desires and magical energy even more than usual. As you write his name, **say the following:**

[Insert his name], by this feather of truth
I here lay upon you this enchantment
That when you are with me, no lies shall pass your lips.
[Insert his name], by this feather of truth
I here lay upon you this enchantment
That you shall never seek to deceive me.

[Insert his name], by this feather of truth
I here lay upon you this enchantment
That you shall never betray me with your words.

When the ink has dried, place the paper in a dictionary, between the pages containing the word "truth."

Q: How can I stop his bad habits?

A. **This has gone on long enough!** You just can't stand it anymore! Whether he bites his nails, whistles tunelessly, or has a list of exaggerated ailments, you know that his bad habits have got to stop. In fact, it's either them or you. But the remedy need not be so drastic. In fact, you already hold the solution in your own hands—your magical prowess. Use your power for this spell and you won't have to grit your teeth at his thoughtless habits again.

Just before bedtime, find a place where he won't disturb you. Take some brittle twigs, one for each bad habit you want to address, and use a black felt-tip pen to write one bad habit on each twig. Bundle up the sticks and place them under the mattress, on his side of the bed; this should ensure that the sticks pick up the energies of the habits named upon them. The next night, at midnight, once again make sure that you are alone. Retrieve the sticks and place them in front of you, along with a clay pot and a black candle. Light the candle and **say:**

His habits, these sticks
These sticks, his habits
Be gone
Be gone
Be gone

His habits, these sticks
These sticks, his habits
Broken
Broken
Broken

Break all of the sticks in half and throw them into the pot. Place the pot by the front door so that when he next enters the house, he will leave his habits there instead of carrying them around with him.

CHECKLIST

Best to use: At midnight, during the waning moon, when you are completely fed up with telling him off for his habits.

How often: Performing this spell just once should do the trick.

You will need:

A brittle twig for each bad habit

A black felt-tip pen

A clay pot

A black candle

Q: We always seem to be fighting. How can I make the peace?

A: **If you are always arguing** and there doesn't seem to be any one cause, maybe it's your surroundings that are at fault. Some houses gather negative energy over the years, which is stored in the very fabric of the walls and floors. Perhaps it is this atmosphere that is fueling the tension between you. To clear your dwelling of such bad vibes, try this cleansing ritual.

Take a dab of olive oil on your finger and anoint a blue candle from the base to the tip. **Repeat these words:**

*I bless this candle of peace that it brings light
and harmony to this house. May all negativity
be cast out before its light.*

Add a drop each of rosemary, vetivert, and juniper essential oils (for positive, protective, and harmonizing energy) to a cup of spring water and drop in a citrine crystal. Swirl the oils around in the water and **say:**

*I bless this water of power that it casts out all shadows,
unhappiness, and anger from this dwelling.*

CHECKLIST
Best to use: During the dark of the moon, just before dawn.
How often: Whenever you feel negative energy gathering around you.

You will need:
Olive oil
A blue candle
A cup of spring water
Rosemary, vetivert, and juniper
  essential oils
A citrine crystal

Take the candle and the water to a place that is roughly in the center of the house. Put down the water and light the candle. Carefully carry the candle through each room of the house, reciting the following words **in each one:**

This light and warmth shall cast out darkness. Be gone, I say, be gone.

Return to the center of the house and place the candle in a safe place. Pick up the water and once more walk through every room, sprinkling the walls and floors with the water as you go. In each room **say:**

> *I cleanse this space of all that is unclean.*
> *Let only happiness and peace reign here. So shall it be.*

Return once more to the center of the house and place the cup by the candle. As dawn breaks, open all the windows in the house to let the light of the new day in, and allow the candle to burn down to a stump.

Q: How can I keep him interested?

A: **You know how it goes.** Suddenly he's spending less time with you and more on his car or buddies. You know he's either losing interest or taking you for granted. Either way, it's time for you to perk up the passion again, so take control and arouse his senses with this magical, mystical perfume of enchantment. It is rather powerful, though, so take care when and where you choose to wear it.

Melt half a teaspoon of wax in a double boiler or a bowl over a saucepan of boiling water, but take care not to get it too hot. Add two tablespoons of almond oil and stir it in well, using a wooden spoon. Now add five drops each of sandalwood, vanilla, patchouli, and vetivert essential oils and stir nine times, **while saying:**

Heaven's scent and honey bee
  Make him want to be with me.
    Nothing else shall there be

Nothing else, only me.
  Heaven's scent and honey bee
As I do will, so shall it be.

Before the mixture cools, take some fresh red rose petals and write a letter of his name on each one. Arrange these at the bottom of a dark glass jar. Pour the perfume mixture into the jar and allow it to cool before placing the cover on top. The heat acting on the initialed rose petals will activate the magic, making a bond between him and you that he'll find hard to ignore. Try wearing some of the perfume on your pulse points the next time his attention is diverted by something far less wonderful than yourself.

Best to use: Make up the perfume on the night before the full moon.

How often:

Make up a fresh batch when you run out and wear as needed.

You will need:

Wax

A double boiler, or a bowl that fits into a saucepan

Almond oil

A wooden spoon

Sandalwood, vanilla, patchouli, and vetivert essential oils

Fresh red rose petals

A pen

A dark glass jar with a cover

Dumpsville

Sometimes, whatever you try to do to save the relationship, it is doomed to failure. Perhaps fate never meant you and he to be. Or maybe you were meant to be together to learn an important life lesson. Now that the lesson has been learned, it is time to move on. Whatever the reason, there is no doubt that breaking up is a hard and painful experience. Of course, you will recover in time, and so will he, but why not employ a helping, soothing, magical hand to heal your heart? Or, if it is you who needs the courage to call things off, you'll find a spell for that here as well.

Q: I've just been dumped. How can I stop hurting?

A: **Even if you didn't have** any real feelings for your ex, being dumped hurts your pride at the very least. However, if you did love him the feelings of heartache are very real indeed, and can last for some time. Of course, you will need to come to terms with the fact that it's over, and lessen any further pain by making sure you see or speak to him as little as possible. But to aid the healing process, make use of magical healing energies that will speed up your recovery and ensure that you soon feel on top of things again.

Light a blue candle and kneel in front of it. Pick up a sponge and hold it to your heart, **while reciting the following:**

I lay this sponge upon my heart.
It shall soak up all my hurt
Until there be no more pain in my heart
And I shall be whole again.
As I do will, so mote it be.

Imagine the hurt leaving your heart as a black, inky substance, and see the sponge soaking it all up. Eventually, when all the pain has been absorbed by the sponge, lay it down and use a black felt-tip pen to draw a smiley face on it. This is to remind you that all will be well in the end. Then, take a piece of string and use it to hang up the sponge outside, where you will be able to see it every morning. As you hang it up, **say the following:**

Rain, wash away my tears
Cleanse my heart of all this hurt.
Breezes, take away my anger

Take away all of my pain.
Sun, warm my frozen feelings
Bring back happiness into my life.

Leave the sponge where it is for at least one month, so that every time you look at it you will remember that it is working for you, erasing your break-up blues day after day.

CHECKLIST

Best to use: During the waning moon, preferably on a Saturday.
How often: You should need to do this only once.

You will need:
A blue candle
A sponge
A black felt-tip pen
String

?Q: How can I learn to trust in love again?

A. When you've been badly hurt in love, you may feel that you'll never trust anyone again. It is only natural to want to take some time out of relationships in order to heal and regain a proper perspective on life. However, if you need a little help with the healing process, try this gentle potion.

Mix together two tablespoons of almond oil and two drops of wheat germ oil in a bowl, to form a base oil. Add three drops each of rose, bergamot, and geranium essential oils and mix by stirring them clockwise with your finger, **saying the following three times:**

> *Potion mix, potion start*
> *Potion blend to heal my heart.*

Decant the oil into a dark glass bottle but leave the cover off. Next, draw an upward-pointing pentagram on some paper and place on your altar. Put the bottle of healing oil on top. Form a triangle around the bottle with one green candle at the back and two white candles at the sides. Light the candles and envision spiraling golden energy being drawn from above and below into the triangle and into the bottle. **Chant:**

CHECKLIST
Best to use: On a Monday, at the new moon.
How often: This wonderfully soothing rite can be used whenever it is needed.

You will need:
Almond oil
Wheat germ oil
Rose, bergamot, and geranium
essential oils
A dark glass bottle with a cover
A sheet of paper and a pen
A green candle
2 white candles

Healing come, healing start
Mend the break across my heart.
Magic powers, below and above
Restore again my trust in love.
For as long as the candles burn,
Let this mill of magic turn.

Let the candles burn out. Put the cover on the bottle, label it, and store in a cool place. Every night, before you sleep, anoint your heart chakra with the oil and **say:**

I heal my heart and trust again.

The oil can also be used as a massage oil, or a few drops can be added to your bath.

Q: I need to ditch my boyfriend but can't find the courage. How do I do it?

A: **Breaking up can be so tough,** especially if you are the caring type who hates to hurt someone else's feelings. Nevertheless, sometimes you just have to bite the bullet and get on with it. Here is a little courage talisman that will help you find the strength to do the dirty deed.

Place two red washcloths together. Draw a heart shape on one and cut the shape out of both fabrics. Stitch the two heart pieces together, leaving a gap about two fingers wide. Stuff the heart with a handful each of St. John's wort, tarragon, and mullein, all said to impart courage, while **chanting the following verse three times:**

Heart be stout
Heart stand firm
I'll do this deed
I will not turn.

Courage surround me
Courage be all
With what is before me
I shall not stall.

Press a carnelian into the center of the bundle—carnelian is a gemstone that gives off powerful energies, which will boost your bravery, ground your fears, and protect you from negativity. Sew up the gap in the heart pouch, then sew some elastic to the sides of the heart—this needs to be long enough to stretch around your rib cage so the heart talisman lies over your solar plexus chakra, just below your diaphragm. Make sure you are wearing the heart when you ditch your man and you will experience an extra boost of bravado.

CHECKLIST

Best to use: On a full moon and preferably on a Tuesday.

How often: Every time you need a little courage, and not necessarily just for dumping your boyfriend.

You will need:

2 red washcloths

Tailor's chalk

Scissors

Needle and thread

St. John's wort, fresh or dried

Tarragon, fresh or dried

Mullein leaf, fresh or dried

A carnelian

Elastic, long enough to fit around your middle

Q: How can I feel good about being single when all my friends are with someone?

A: **Do you spend nights** feeling lonely and unloved because all your friends are in relationships, and you're not? The chances are that those friends who are in long-term relationships are actually envying you your freedom. But that's no help when you have the lonesome blues. Try this empowering self-affirmation ritual to make you feel positively single.

Arrange to have a night free of interruptions. Avoid the television, take the phone off the hook, and forget the housework. Prepare the room you will do this ritual in by laying everything you need on a low altar with a cushion in front of it. Decorate the room with extra candles or flowers—be extravagant, remember you are honoring you! Prepare yourself by having a long, scented, candlelit bath before dressing in your favorite clothes, makeup, and jewelry. Sit on the cushion and light two violet candles and your favorite incense. Place a garland of flowers on your head. Fill a goblet with red wine and look into it. As you stare into its blood-red depths, visualize everything you can do without having to worry about someone else's feelings or plans. Maybe you see yourself shopping without having to worry about the inquisition when you get home. Or watching your favorite television show without interruption. When you have exhausted your daydreams, **say:**

I am queen of my own universe,
Ruler of my destiny.
I am at one with the sun and the
moon and the stars.
All of nature is
in me.

I am content with what I have
And I trust in a higher power that
all is as it should be.
I now claim my right to happiness
As I dance toward the wonderful
future that awaits me.

Drink the wine and spend the evening thinking of all the amazing things that have happened so far in your life. Of the battles you have fought and won, or lost and learned from. Remind yourself how wonderful you are!

CHECKLIST

Best to use: Any time you are on your own and feeling a bit low.
How often: No limits. Use to boost your self-esteem as often as you need to.

You will need:
A cushion
2 violet candles
Your favorite incense stick and an incense stick holder
A garland of flowers
A goblet of red wine

Q: I want the relationship to end but for us to to remain friends. What can I do?

A: So you've realized that you'd be better off as friends instead of lovers. Well, it's all very well to say that, but it is not so easy to make it happen. All breakups tend to involve a degree of hurt or bruised pride, and parted lovers often prefer to go their separate ways entirely, rather than remain chummy on a daily basis. However, if you are still determined to be pals with your ex, smooth the way with this spell.

Stand two white tapers firmly in some soil in a small plant pot. Stretch three strands of red cotton and one of white between the tapers, tying the ends of the cotton to the tapers. Visualize one taper as yourself and the other as the person you wish to break up with. See the cotton as the emotional ties that bind you together. When the image is firmly fixed in your mind, light the tapers and pick up a pair of scissors. Repeat the following and cut the red cotton strands **as directed:**

These ties that bind me and thee
I shall cut, to set us free.
Eye to eye, this bond is broken
[cut one red strand]
Body to body, this bond is broken
[cut one red strand]
Heart to heart, this bond is

broken [cut the last red strand]
This bond I leave is that of friend
But all else we had is at an end.
Love's fires die and
friendship grow
As I will, it shall be so.

Let the tapers burn down and bury all that is left—strands and wax—at the bottom of the pot of soil. Place a piece of rose quartz, stone of friendship, on the top. Finally, plant some sweet pea seeds according to the instructions on the packet; if you can't get sweet peas, any

flower you like can be substituted. Then nurture the plants and watch your new friendship grow as your relationship ends.

CHECKLIST

Best to use: Perform this spell at the new moon.

How often: You will need to do this only once.

You will need:
2 white wax tapers
A small soil-filled plant pot
3 strands of red cotton
1 strand of white cotton
Scissors
A small piece of rose quartz
Sweet pea seeds

Q: How can I get my man back again?

A. **You miss him! You want him!** You can't sleep or eat without him! In fact you simply can't live without him by your side. Maybe you've tried everything to get over the breakup, but still feel that somehow you and he were meant to be. Well, if you're really that desperate to get him back, try this spell, and if there is even the slightest hint of magic between you, you'll soon find him in your arms again.

Ideally, this ritual is best performed out of doors, in a secluded spot. First, draw out a circle of approximately 9 feet (2.5–3 m) in diameter on the ground, either by scratching it into the earth or forming it with stones, twigs, or salt. Put the four red candles into jars (to stop them going out), light them, and place them and four patchouli incense sticks at the quarter points of the circle: north, south, east, and west. Place a photograph of your ex (or other item), in the middle of the circle with a magnet on top and light the candles. Step into the circle and slowly begin to walk in a clockwise (deosil) direction, **chanting:**

As I do will,
so shall it be
[Insert his name],
you will come back to me

Circle round
Lost and found
The spell is cast
This magic will last.

Repeat this three times, then repeat the last two lines over and over again, getting louder and louder as you speed your pace. Once you are running, slow down again to a walk and quiet your voice to a whisper. At this point, stop and sink to the floor. See and feel the power you have raised swirling in a large, silvery cone above the center of the circle. Stand up, take hold of it, and throw it up to the heavens where it can do its work. Tidy up after

yourself and make sure you leave the area as you found it. When you get
home, hang the magnet outside your house like a beacon for his return.

CHECKLIST

Best to use: Perform this spell
on the full moon, in good weather
if working outdoors.

How often: Once only. It would
be unethical to push too hard
against his free will to choose
who he loves.

You will need:

A large stick or some stones,
  twigs, or salt
4 red candles
4 patchouli incense sticks and 4
  incense stick holders
A photograph of the man in
  question or other item belonging
  to him
A magnet

Q: How can I turn my ex into a toad?

A: **Does he deserve everything** that's coming to him? Wouldn't you just like to turn him into a toad? Well, of course, literally turning him into a toad isn't possible, no matter how magically proficient you are. But with this spell you should be able to make him display the meaner side of his nature to everyone.

Mold some air-drying clay into the best toadlike shape you can muster, and leave to dry. When it has thoroughly hardened, place a little water in a mixing bowl. Add flour until it forms a lumpy paste, then tear some newspaper into small pieces. Dip the newspaper pieces into the flour paste until they are evenly covered and apply them to the clay in an even layer. Let this layer dry before adding another, final covering. When the second layer is dry, take a picture of your ex and write his full name on the back three times. Then tear up the picture, dip it in the paste, and put it on your "toad." **Say:**

[Insert his name], true nature no longer be hidden,
Your toadish side is now bidden
To show itself to everyone,
To spoil everybody's fun.

For all the hurt you gave to me
I send it back to you, times three.
Then what you do and what you say
Will make people turn away.

When the picture is dry, paint the toad green with a black mouth and eyes. Keep the toad for no longer than a month, and in a place where you can see it and feel smug. Once the month is up, you must free your ex from this spell by smashing the toad. As you bury the pieces, **say:**

[Insert his name], you are freed from this spell.
Learn your lesson and live your life well.

CHECKLIST

Best to use: Let loose this enchantment at the full moon.

How often: Once is enough to teach him a short, sharp lesson.

You will need:
Some air-drying clay
A mixing bowl
Flour
Newspaper
A photograph or drawing of the man in question
Green and black poster paint

?Q: How can I stop my ex from spreading rumors about me?

A: **Your relationship may be over,** but your problems aren't. You've been hearing some nasty gossip about yourself recently and there's only one source it could have come from—your ex. You could confront him directly and ask him to stop, but if this doesn't work, use this spell to stop him badmouthing you once and for all.

At the top of a sheet of black paper, write your ex's name in white chalk. Underneath, write the name again, but this time with the end letter missing. Continue reducing his name in the same way until you are left with only one letter. Diminishing someone's name is very strong magic in itself, because it lessens that person's power. Take the paper outside and dig a hole. Lay the paper in the hole and place a piece of hematite and a small mirror—to reflect back his bad intentions—on top. Stab each corner of the paper with a cocktail stirrer, pinning it into the earth, while visualizing your ex and **repeating these words:**

By wood and earth, I hold you down.
By this spell, you are bound to spread no lies about me
No gossip or rumors shall come from thee.
All of your bad words shall cease and between us shall be only peace.

Heap earth over the top of the hole until it forms a mound. Leave enough time for the paper to rot away before retrieving the hematite and mirror, unless you wish to leave them there.

CHECKLIST

Best to use: During the dark of the moon and preferably on a Saturday.

How often: This is a powerful spell so use only once and in an emergency.

You will need:

A sheet of black paper

White chalk

A piece of hematite

A small mirror

4 cocktail stirrers

Basic magical knowledge

To ensure that a spell works you need your strength of will, but to concoct a spell of your own you also need some basic knowledge of the properties and energies of our magical "helpers." For example, during which phase of the moon should you perform a spell aimed at attracting a mate? What color candle should you use to bring happiness into your life?

To come to grips with this basic knowledge, look no further than the following lists of sources of magical energy that can be used for any kind of magic, not necessarily just the romantic kind.

ELEMENTS

The elements of air, earth, fire, and water have been used in magic for thousands of years. The ancients taught that the universe was made up of these four elements, plus one other: spirit. Like everything else, they possess magical energy that, when used in the right way, can add power to your spells.

Earth This element, represented by rocks, soil, and plants, symbolizes stability and solidity. Its energy is useful in grounding magical energy, money spells, and spells to protect the environment.

Air Air energy is carried by the wind, incense, birds (feathers), and trees. It is very much the energy of the mind, of clear thought, communication, inspiration, news, and prayers.

Fire Fire's flame is represented in spells by candles; just having a candle present in your ritual will increase its energy. The element of fire is associated with passion, power, creative energy, and sexuality.

Water Water connects us to the subconscious, the emotions, and our dreams, as well as opening up a link into other worlds. It can also be used in purification and healing work.

DAYS OF THE WEEK

The days of the week are ruled by different planets, and therefore have their own special energies.

Sunday	Ruled by the sun. A good day for spells for healing and general happiness.
Monday	Ruled by the moon. This day is propitious for psychic work, divination, healing, and women's magic.
Tuesday	Ruled by Mars. Tuesday's energy has to do with resolving conflicts and getting rid of fears.
Wednesday	Ruled by Mercury. This is a day for communication magic and anything to do with travel or career.
Thursday	Ruled by Jupiter. A good day for good luck, justice, abundance, and everything working out.
Friday	Ruled by Venus. The best day to do love magic, create friendships, or bring harmony and peace into your life.
Saturday	Ruled by Saturn. A good day for banishing and binding and for getting rid of things that hinder your life's path.

MOON PHASES

Different phases of the moon's cycle also benefit different kinds of magic.

New moon	This is the best time for new beginnings.
Waxing moon	Good for magic that will have a positive outcome or something to be gained.
Full moon	A time of completion, of bringing everything together. Also good for divination.
Waning moon	A time for banishing and binding magic. A good period to release unwanted things from your life and psyche.

COLORS

You can make use of the energies of colors by using colored candles or pouches. Here is a list of the basic colors and the kinds of energy they create.

Red	Passion, lust, physical energy, courage, and protection.
Orange	Creativity, communication, intellect, and career.
Yellow/gold	Health and happiness.
Green	Harmony, wealth, and fidelity.
Blue	Abundance, justice, healing, and harmony.
Pink	True love, friendship, and peace.
Purple	Higher spiritual energies for psychic work.
Silver/violet	Psychic work, healing, and divination.
Black	Getting rid of negative energies, and binding and banishing spells.
White	All magical purposes as well as healing, purity, and peace.

SYMBOLS

Symbols have been used for centuries to represent different energies or to convey meanings. Some symbols (as below) are specific to love magic.

Pentagram	Prime magical symbol that represents the union of the four elements, plus spirit.
Star of Venus	Ancient symbol of the evening star, associated in many cultures with the goddess of love.
Astrological sign for Venus	The symbol used to denote the planet Venus, associated in astrology and alchemy with love.

INGREDIENTS SPECIFIC TO LOVE MAGIC

The following lists of love spell ingredients are by no means exhaustive. If you wish to explore further, there are many good magical herbal and crystal guides on the market.

Herbs & plants for love Apple, apricot, basil, calendula, caraway, chamomile, cherry blossom, coriander, daisy, dill, elecampane, geranium, honey-suckle, jasmine, lavender, lemon balm, lotus, myrtle, pansy, rose, rosemary, southernwood, valerian, vanilla, vervain, yarrow.

Herbs & plants for lust Acorn, avocado, cinnamon, clove, fig, ginger, ginseng, hibiscus, mint, southernwood, vanilla.

Crystals & stones

Agate (truth)
Amber (unconditional love, healing)
Amethyst (heals broken hearts)
Beryl (attracts love, forgiveness)
Carnelian (passion, vitality)
Citrine (cleansing, calm, and happiness)
Diamond (eternal love)
Fluorite (seeing things clearly, increases libido)
Garnet (passion, affection, friendship)
Hematite (protection)

Jade (eternal love and commitment)
Jasper (passion, nurturing)
Lapis lazuli (spiritual love, truth)
Lodestone (attracts love)
Quartz (stores energy)
Rose quartz (romantic love, friendship, affection)
Ruby (deep love, passion, protection)
Sodalite (emotional balance)
Tiger's eye (confidence)
Topaz (happiness, truth)
Turquoise (friendships, inner strength)

Scents and incense Cedarwood, frankincense, jasmine, musk, neroli, patchouli, rose, rosewood, sandalwood, vanilla, ylang ylang.

Index

Thanks (first and foremost!) to my mum—for believing in me and for always being there when I need her. To my daughter, Ellie—who is my constant inspiration and shining light. To Tony, who came into my life to teach me a necessary lesson about how much I was worth. To Beverley and Sharon— for being marvelous friends and sharing the coffee, laughter, and tears (not necessarily in that order!). To Sharon and Alan, locked away in the attic at Dunholme, for listening to my rants. To the folks at L.A. for keeping me fit (especially Pauline and Alec). To Kate and Jo at Quarto, for keeping me mostly sane. And to my spirit guides and helpers for never letting me down. Finally, I open my arms wide to all those wonderful people in my future whom I have yet to have the pleasure of meeting and knowing.